MW00760492

THIS BOOK

BELONGS TO

Heart's Witness

A WEDDING BOOK

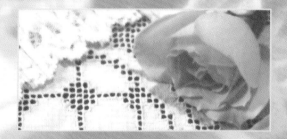

Edited by Sarah Weir

Ariel Books

Andrews and McMeel
Kansas City

Heart's Witness: A Wedding Book copyright © 1995 by Armand Eisen. All rights reserved. Printed in Singapore. No part of this book may be used or reproduced in any manner whatsoever without written permission except in the case of reprints in the context of reviews. For information write Andrews and McMeel, a Universal Press Syndicate Company, 4900 Main Street, Kansas City, Missouri 64112.

The text of this book was set in Eva Antiqua with display in Nuptial by
M Space, Brooklyn, New York

Book design by Maura Fadden Rosenthal

ISBN 0-8362-4745-0

Photographic images by Maura Fadden Rosenthal. Art Credits: p. 18: W. Savage Cooper, *Betrothed*, n.d.; p. 25: George Godwin Kilburne, *The Wedding Dress*, n.d.; p.38: William Dyce, *Paolo and Francesca*, 1837.

CONTENTS

INTRODUCTION

The power of love is awesome. Perhaps this is why weddings, the public expression of love, remain an essential rite of passage where other rituals have faded or ceased to exist altogether. Weddings are joyful occasions. The most restrained of us beam with delight and the most sophisticated of us weep tears of joy.

The wedding ritual is a bond with the past, linking us to traditions born many centuries ago. It is also a connection to the future: the beginning of a new life for two people sharing the same path, extending the family, and forging new ties.

The wedding is a great pageant—the most elaborately staged production most brides- and grooms-to-be will ever participate in and one in which couples can feel temporarily set adrift in the swirl of events and preparations. At such times, a dip into this lovely volume may provide moments of relief. It unearths the meaning behind traditions that might otherwise seem oddly out of date. It offers love poems and wedding lore for reflection. And it helps you pause and become your own heart's witness as you are swept on a journey of love.

Heart's Witness

TRUE LOVE

❧❧

THE POETS
SPEAK

*I*t is difficult to know at what moment love begins; it is less

difficult to know that it has begun.

—Henry Wadsworth Longfellow

*F*rom exchanging glances, they advance to acts of courtesy,

of gallantry, then to fiery passion, to plighting troth and

marriage. Passion beholds its object as a perfect unit. The soul

is wholly embodied, and the body is wholly ensouled.

—Ralph Waldo Emerson

A Wedding Book

> Heart, are you great enough
>
> for a love that never tires?
>
> O heart, are you great enough for love?
>
> —Alfred, Lord Tennyson

On December 10, 1936, King Edward VIII gave up the British throne in order to marry Wallis Simpson, an American divorcée. "I have found it impossible to carry my heavy burden of responsibility and to discharge my duties as King as I wish to do," he told his subjects, "without the help and support of the woman I love."

Love is that splendid triggering of human vitality . . . the supreme activity which nature affords anyone for going out of himself toward someone else.

—José Ortega y Gasset

Heart's Witness

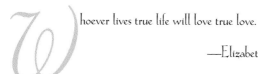
hoever lives true life will love true love.

—Elizabeth Barrett Browning

any waters cannot quench love, neither can the floods drown it.

—Song of Solomon 8:7

f you love me as I love you
What knife can cut our love in two?

—Rudyard Kipling

A Birthday

My heart is like a singing bird
    Whose nest is in a watered shoot:
My heart is like an apple-tree
    Whose boughs are bent with thickset fruit;
My heart is like a rainbow shell
    That paddles in a halcyon sea;
My heart is gladder than all these
    Because my love is come to me.

Raise me on a dais of silk and down;
    Hang it with vair and purple dyes;
Carve it in doves and pomegranates,
    And peacocks with a hundred eyes;
Work it in gold and silver grapes
    In leaves and silver fleurs-de-lys;
Because the birthday of my life
    Is come, my love is come to me.

—Christina Rossetti

A Book of Verses underneath the Bough,
A Jug of Wine, a Loaf of Bread—and Thou
Beside me singing in the Wilderness—
Oh, Wilderness were Paradise enow!

—Edward FitzGerald,
tr. of the "Rubáiyát of Omar Khayyám"

This is one of the miracles of love: It gives . . . a power
of seeing through its own enchantments and yet not
being disenchanted.

—C. S. Lewis

Love is the May-day of the heart.

—Benjamin Disraeli

Nature is fine in love: and where 'tis fine,
It sends some precious instance of itself
After the thing it loves.

—William Shakespeare, *Hamlet*

Lyric Love, half angel and half bird,
And all a wonder and a wild desire.

—Robert Browning

There is nothing holier, in this life of ours, than the first
consciousness of love—the first fluttering of its silken
wings.

—Henry Wadsworth Longfellow

THE PROPOSAL

*T*wo we are, and one we'll be,

If you consent to marry me.

—Anonymous

Is there any other question that sets hearts pounding like *"Will you marry me?"* Even if a couple has previously discussed getting married, the proposal is sure to cause cheeks to blush, hands to shake, and stomachs to flutter. Suddenly life is refreshed; everything shimmers in a world now shared by two.

Proposals have no set pattern. The male suitor on bended knee asking his loved one for her hand in marriage may be a gallant and romantic image, but it doesn't often happen that way. Proposals are as unique as the people who make them. Any moment can be the right moment to "pop the question," whether it is planned in advance or asked spontaneously—perhaps even simultaneously.

Of course, it is not always the male suitor who proposes. Queen Victoria, who was queen of the United Kingdom from 1837 to her death in 1901, wrote the following passage in her journal on October 15, 1839. She and Albert of Saxe-Coburg-Gotha married on February 10, 1840.

> . . . after a few minutes I said to him, that I thought he must be aware why I wished [him] to come here, and that it would make me too happy if he would consent to what I wished (to marry me); we embraced each other over and over again, and he was so kind, so affectionate; Oh! to feel I was, and am, loved by such an Angel as Albert was too great delight to describe! he is perfection; perfection in every way—in beauty—in everything! I told him I was quite unworthy of him and kissed his dear hand—he said he would be very happy [to share his life with her] and was so kind and seemed so happy, that I really felt it was the happiest brightest moment in my life . . . Oh! how I adore and love him, I cannot say!! . . . I feel the happiest of human beings.

Suddenly she said to him with extraordinary beauty: "I engage myself to you forever."

The beauty was in everything, and he could have separated nothing—couldn't have thought of her face as distinct from the whole joy. Yet her face had a new light. "And I pledge you—I call God to witness!—every spark of my faith; I give you every drop of my life." That was all, for the moment, but it was enough, ... They had exchanged vows and tokens, sealed their rich compact, solemnised, so far as breathed words and murmured sounds and lighted eyes and clasped hands could do it, their agreement to belong only, and to belong tremendously, to each other.

—Henry James, *The Wings of the Dove*

My most brilliant achievement was my ability to be able to persuade my wife to marry me.

—Winston Churchill

Somebody at my elbow suggests that I have not intimated how a man should propose. The plain truth is I do not know. But a man must not be abject. Faint heart never won fair lady since the world began.

—Margaret E. Sangster, *Good Manners for All Occasions*

A Pledge That Sparkles

Only recently have brides worn both an engagement ring and a wedding band. Long ago, couples exchanged betrothal rings which symbolized a contract more binding than today's engagement. Originally, betrothal rings were crafted of bronze, bone, iron, or even dried rushes. These materials eventually gave way to silver, gold, and platinum set with precious stones. Finally, in the fifteenth century, diamonds became popular for betrothal rings because their beauty and strength were thought to bring the wearer enduring love.

Love is a circle that doth restless move
In the same sweet eternity of love.

—Robert Herrick

The fountains mingle with the river,
    And the rivers mingle with the ocean;
The winds of heaven mix forever,
    With a sweet emotion;
Nothing in the world is single,
    All things by a law divine
In one another's being mingle—
    Why not I with thine?

—Percy Bysshe Shelley

A popular type of betrothal ring in the late Renaissance was the gimmal ring. The gimmal ring contained two bands joined with a decorative clasp. The bands could be separated, one for the bride-to-be and one for her fiancé. Another type of gimmal ring was made with three bands—the third band was meant for a witness to the betrothal. The exchange of rings in modern wedding ceremonies with the best man as witness hearkens back to the betrothal ritual.

THE WEDDING DAY

*T*he sun-beams in the east are spread,

     Leave, leave, fair Bride, your solitary bed,

     No more shall you return to it alone, . . .

Come glad from thence, go gladder than you came,

Today put on perfection, and a woman's name.

                           —John Donne

Whether traditional or free-spirited, every wedding seems transported from a fairy tale and every bride a princess. The bride and groom are bestowed with tranquil joy and all nervousness is washed away. The guests hush to witness the same ancient rituals enacted for generations. In this respect, there is no such thing as a modern wedding—a man and woman united in love is a timeless occurrence.

When to Wed?

June and September are the most popular months for marriages, but in earlier times an old rhyme might have proved helpful in picking the date:

Married when the year is new,

He'll be loving, kind and true.

When February birds do mate

You wed nor dread your fate.

If you were wed when March winds blow,

Joy and sorrow both you'll know.

Marry in April when you can

Joy for maiden and the man.

Marry in the month of May

And you'll surely rue the day.

Marry when June roses grow

Over land and sea you'll go.

Those who in July do wed

Must labour for their daily bread.

Whoever wed in August be,

Many a change is sure to see.

Marry in September's shine,

Your living will be rich and fine.

If in October you do marry

Love will come, but riches tarry.

If you wed in bleak November

Only joys will come, remember.

When December's snows fall fast,

Marry and true love will last.

—Anonymous

lest is the bride on whom the sun doth shine.

—Robert Herrick

It is lucky to marry when the moon is full and when the tide is high.

—Irish proverb

What to Wear

Though brides wore white robes in ancient times, the classic, frothy white wedding gown only came into vogue in the nineteenth century. Prior to that, a European or American bride simply donned her best dress, probably the one she wore to church on Sunday. Though these ensembles were often in creamy shades of yellow, lilac, or rose, very pious brides preferred darker colors. Even today, the white wedding dress is by no means universal. In China brides wear red, the color of good fortune; in India brides interlace their gowns with golden threads; and until recently, Icelandic brides wore black. Perhaps many brides were guided by the following verse popular during the Victorian era:

Married in gray, you will go far away.

Married in black, you will wish yourself back.

Married in brown, you will live out of town.

Married in red, you will wish yourself dead.

Married in pearl, you will live in a whirl.

Married in green, ashamed to be seen.

Married in yellow, ashamed of your fellow.

Married in blue, he will always be true.

Married in pink, your spirits will sink.

Married in white, you have chosen aright.

When Grace Kelly married His Serene Highness Rainier III in Monaco, her flower girls wore Mary Janes and ankle socks from the J. C. Penney catalog. You don't need to spend a king's ransom to wed in style.

Something Old, Something New

For centuries brides have been advised to carry "Something old, something new, something borrowed, something blue," on their wedding day. While the rhyme may seem trite, the underlying sentiment poignantly reflects a bride's feelings on her wedding day. Something old represents continuity with the past; something new, anticipation and hope for the future; something borrowed (ideally from a happily married friend), good luck; and something blue, purity and love.

A Veil . . .

When Major Lawrence Lewis was courting Nellie Custis, daughter of George and Martha Washington, one day he commented how pretty she looked sitting behind a lace-curtained window. Remembering this compliment on her wedding day, Nellie single-handedly brought a now familiar tradition to America: she married in a veil.

And a Train . . .

When Lady Diana Spencer married Prince Charles on July 28, 1981, her dress was trailed by a twenty-five foot silk train.

Meg looked very like a rose herself; for all that was best and sweetest in heart and soul seemed to bloom into her face that day, making it fair and tender, with a charm more beautiful than beauty. Neither silk, lace, nor orange-flowers would she have. "I don't want a fashionable wedding, but only those about me whom I love, and to them I wish to look and be my familiar self."

—Louisa May Alcott, *Good Wives*

The Bouquet

In early times, the bridal bouquet was made of bitter herbs. Once in her new home, the young wife burned the herbs to release a pungent smoke and drive away bad spirits. Eventually, brides carried sweeter and more decorative herbs like lavender and thyme. By the time of the Renaissance, orange blossoms, symbolizing purity, had become the most popular flower for the bridal bouquet.

Other flowers commonly used in wedding bouquets have traditional meanings as well.

Calla Lily ❧ *beauty*

Baby's Breath ❧ *innocence*

Lily of the Valley ❧ *sweetness*

Orchid ❧ *fertility*

White Violet ❧ *opportunity*

Blue Violet ❧ *faithfulness*

Gardenia ❧ *joy*

Heather ❧ *admiration*

Rose ❧ *love*

Daffodil ❧ *respect*

Aster ❧ *delicacy*

A Plain Gold Band

I would like to have engraved inside every wedding band *Be kind to one another.* This is the Golden Rule of marriage and the secret of making love last through the years.

—Randolph Ray, *My Little Church Around the Corner*

By the sixteenth and seventeenth centuries, gold wedding bands had surpassed betrothal rings in popularity. So many couples favored the exchange of gold rings that it became a necessary part of the marriage vows. Even country priests kept a few bands available for poor peasant couples to borrow during the ceremony. An ancient tradition called for the ring to be slipped onto the third finger of the left hand, from which a vein runs straight to the heart.

Heart's Witness

To thee this ring,

    Made for thy finger fit;

To show by this

That our love is

    Or should be, like to it.

And as this round

Is nowhere found

    To flaw, or else to sever,

So let our love

As endless prove,

    And pure as gold forever.

                  —Robert Herrick

During the Roman Empire, it was the ceremonial kiss that made the marriage binding, not an exchange of rings.

The Blessing

For what thou art is mine:

Our state cannot be sever'd; we are one,

One flesh; to lose thee were to lose myself.

—John Milton, *Paradise Lost*

Once the couple exchanges rings and is pronounced husband and wife, blessings are bestowed upon their union, as in the following.

↢ Blessed are you, Holy one of the Cosmos, who makes the bridegroom and bride to rejoice.

↢ Blessed are you, Holy One of All, who created joy and gladness, bride and bridegroom, mirth and song, pleasure and delight, love, fellowship, peace, and friendship. . . .

—from the Hebrew Seven Blessings

Now you will feel no rain,

for each of you will be a shelter to the other.

Now you will feel no cold,

for each of you will be warmth to the other.

Now there is no loneliness for you;

now there is no more loneliness.

Now you are two bodies,

but there is only one life before you.

Go now to your dwelling place,

to enter into your days together.

And may your days be good

and long on the earth.

—Traditional Apache song

We have taken the seven steps. You have become mine forever. Yes, we have become partners. I have become yours. Hereafter, I cannot live without you. Do not live without me. Let us share the joys. We are word and meaning, united. You are thought and I am sound.

May the nights be honey-sweet for us; may the mornings be honey-sweet for us; may the earth be honey-sweet for us; may the heavens be honey-sweet for us.

May the plants be honey-sweet for us; may the sun be all honey for us; may the cows yield us honey-sweet milk!

As the heavens are stable, as the earth is stable, as the mountains are stable, as the whole universe is stable, so may our union be permanently settled.

—from the Hindu marriage ritual of the "Seven Steps"

THE CELEBRATION

I sing of brooks, of blossoms, birds, and bowers,
   Of April, May, of June, and July flowers;
   I sing of Maypoles, Hock-carts, wassails, wakes,
Of bridegrooms, brides, and of their bridal cakes.

—Robert Herrick

Throw off your shoes and dance! The wedding party is a time for unbridled celebration. In medieval times, feasting often lasted for a month. Friends and family welcome the newlyweds into married life and offer them heartfelt toasts and blessings. The bride and groom spin, breathless, through the first dance. With such romance in the air, a few more matches are likely to be made. . . .

The Wedding Cake

The wedding cake, tiered and richly decorated, or simple and elegant, stands as the focus of a celebratory feast. Through the first half of the twentieth century, couples preferred fruitcake with a hard sugar frosting. Often baked days before the actual wedding, the icing could become so hard that one etiquette manual even suggested the bride cut the cake with a saw!

Modern wedding cakes are as varied as the tastes they are made to satisfy. Some are white, some chocolate; some are decorated with delicate flowers of icing, some surrounded with fresh, miniature roses. However they look, and whatever they are made of, when the bride and groom feed each other that first bite, they symbolically feed each other love—and a promise to nurture and support each other in the years to come.

After her wedding to Prince Aly Khan, actress Rita Hayworth cut her wedding cake with a glass sword.

Wedding Cake Wisdom

❀ Good fortune will shine on those couples who save a piece of their wedding cake to share on their first anniversary. (Perhaps this is why long-lasting fruitcakes were so popular before the advent of modern freezing methods.)

❀ Brides who taste the cake before it is cut lose their husband's love.

❀ A bride should pass a bit of cake through her wedding ring to ensure a lasting match.

❀ Bridesmaids who sleep with a bit of cake under their pillow will dream of their true love.

❀ When the first daughter weds, a piece of the wedding cake should be kept by her parents to ensure the marriage of all their daughters.

Toasts

God, the best maker of all marriages,

Combine your hearts in one.

—William Shakespeare, *Henry V*

Laugh and be merry together, like brothers akin,

Guesting awhile in the room of a beautiful inn.

Glad till the dancing stops, and the lilt of the music ends.

Laugh till the game is played; and be you merry my friends.

—John Masefield

Let all thy joys be as the month of May,

And all thy days be as a marriage day:

Let sorrow, sickness, and a troubled mind

Be stranger to thee.

—Francis Quarles

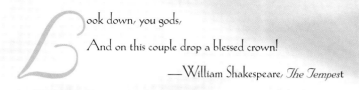

*L*ook down, you gods,
And on this couple drop a blessed crown!
—William Shakespeare, *The Tempest*

*M*ay your hands be forever clasped in friendship
and your hearts joined forever in love.
—Anonymous

Just Married

After exchanging vows and receiving the officiate's blessing, the just-married couple goes through rituals to welcome them into wedded life.

In America guests toss rice, a symbol of fertility, on the newlyweds. In France they shower the couple with wheat, and in Morocco, with dried fruit. The bride then tosses her bouquet into the crowd of well-wishers. With this gesture, she transfers her good fortune in marriage to the person who catches it—said to be the next to wed.

Less common now, but imperative in earlier times, is the tossing of the garter. First the best man slips the just-married bride's garter off her leg in as gallant a fashion as possible. Before the sixteenth century, when priests outlawed the practice at church weddings, the groomsmen seized the bride, scooped her up, and tore the garter from her thigh.

Couples often leave the site of their reception in a car festooned with streamers and balloons, and often trailed by old shoes. This custom probably comes from the Near East where in ancient times an exchange of slippers marked the end of a successful business transaction. Though today's bride marries for love, the shoes echo a time when marriages were arranged by families.

HAPPILY
EVER AFTER

The wedding ceremony is the ritual transition for two people from their lives as singles to their life together. It marks the beginning of their joint path, their decision to travel together. And what comes after? These poets and writers have some thoughts on being married.

A good marriage is that in which each appoints the other guardian of his solitude. Once the realization is accepted that even between the *closest* human beings infinite distances continue to exist, a wonderful living side by side can grow up, if they succeed in loving the distance between them which makes it possible for each to see the other whole against the sky.

—Rainer Maria Rilke

*I*n a successful marriage, there is no such thing as one's way. There is only the way of both, only the bumpy, dusty, difficult, but always mutual path!

—Phyllis McGinley

*M*arriage hath in it less of beauty, but more of safety than the single life; it hath more care, but less danger; it is more merry, and more sad; is fuller of sorrows, and fuller of joys: it lies under more burdens, but is supported by all the strengths of love and charity, and those burdens are delightful.

—Jeremy Taylor, *Twenty-Seven Sermons*

A happy marriage has in it all the pleasures of friendship, all the enjoyments of sense and reason; and indeed all the sweets of life.

—Joseph Addison